MW01142203

Wisdom at Work

Confucian Ideals

&

Japanese
Business Success

DR. TOSHIO ITOH

Fithian Press
SANTA BARBARA
1992

Design and typography by Jim Cook

Published by Fithian Press
Post Office Box 1525
Santa Barbara, California 93102

LIBRARY OF CONGRESS CATALOGING-IN-PUBLICATION DATA
Ito, Tohio, 1932–
    Wisdom at work: Confucian ideals and Japanese business success /
Tohio Itoh.
        p.   cm.
    Based on his book published in Japanese.
    ISBN 1-56474-023-4
    1. Psychology, Industrial—Japan—Religious aspects—Confucianism.
2. Success in business—Japan—Psychological aspects. I. Title.
HF5548.8.I84   1992   92-497
158.7'0952—dc20   CIP

Contents

To my respective friends in MELCO
and my wife.

Foreword

In analyzing the society and the mind of the modern Japanese in this book, Dr. Toshio Itoh refers to the sayings of Confucius, which are collected in the book *Analects of Confucius*—called *Rongo* in Japanese.

In order to explain my understanding of Dr. Itoh's references to the Analects, it is necessary that I first introduce my own understanding of Rongo. Rongo is very popular in Japan, and many Japanese maxims are derived from it. Therefore, it is a useful book from which business executives can gain an understanding of the minds of customers and employees.

I like Rongo very much. While Confucius—the *Master* in Rongo—is the most respected Asian philosopher and teacher, he is regarded neither as a sage nor as a charismatic man. The following story shows why:

> Confucius made a mistaken decision, which led him and his disciples into trouble. One of his disciples blamed Confucius for the mistake, saying, "Does it happen that a Gentleman falls into serious trouble?" Confucius replied,

"Of course he does. But he is a petty person who loses his composure when in trouble."

This story tells us that Confucius made mistakes, sometimes worried, and was sometimes resentful. However, he was so great that, throughout his life, he never forgot loyalty to and consideration for others.

Rongo teaches us how we should behave as good citizens, and instructs us how we should manage people. On one hand, Rongo is a book for the "man in the street," while on the other it is a book for statesmen and managers. I have read many modern management books that were published in the United States. It is my opinion that Rongo is far more practical than these.

Dr. Itoh is an engineer. I have kept my eye on him since I was made a vice president of Mitsubishi Electric Corporation. He worked in the Central Research Laboratory when he was young, and invented many new products and managed projects to develop and sell those products. Many of these products are still made and sold by Mitsubishi Electric today.

In 1979, Dr. Itoh was transferred to our Nagoya works, where for several years he was manager of the Product Development Department and successfully led the development of many new products. Many of these products have been made and sold, profiting Mitsubishi. Dr. Itoh became the general manager of our Manufacturing Development Laboratory in the early 1980s, and then general manager of our Central Research Laboratory, both of which he managed very well.

Dr. Itoh used his leisure time to write a book, *Kite,* and was awarded a prize by the New York Academy of Science.

Engineers in charge of research and development generally have strong egos, and it is difficult to lead them toward a common goal. Why was Dr. Itoh so good at leading these engineers? I found the answer by reading the Japanese version of his book. He led his engineers by the precepts of Rongo.

I, too, have unconsciously applied the concepts of Rongo to manage my company. I read Rongo when I was young and am well aware of the concepts it teaches. For example, I have said to section managers, "If you want to get good results, accomplish your job quickly. The quicker the accomplishment, the more effective the achievement." Confucius said,

> A Gentleman is prompt in his accomplishment. . . . A fast accomplishment results in a prominent achievement.

I have said to department managers, "Do not require your workers to give you frequent reviews of their proposals. If you participate in the review process, then you can get a satisfactory result after two revisions." Confucius said,

> Carry out a task after reviewing it twice. Three times is too often.

I have said to directors, "Make decisions to pay money quickly if you have to pay eventually. You will give a good impression to the person to whom you owe money." Confucius said,

> To be unwilling to spend money that must be spent eventually is the mind-set of a petty official, not a minister.

And I have said to everybody, "Say your opinion positively." Confucius said,

> You are thought to be a tricky man hiding something if

you do not speak when you should. . . . A virtuous person speaks his opinion positively. . . . A Gentleman behaves with harmony, but makes objections if he believes it necessary.

I imagine that many Japanese managers use the precepts of Rongo for management, as do Dr. Itoh and I.

I hope that this book will help people in the United States understand the thinking of Japanese people.

SADAKAZU SHINDO
Former chairman
Mitsubishi Electric Corporation

Introduction

When I became a manager in the research laboratory at Mitsubishi Electric Corporation, I thought to myself, "We Japanese are completely free today. Do we therefore behave just as we like? No, we live and work according to a certain system of morality. Generally, it is a religion that supplies this system. However, most Japanese people are indifferent to religion—at least today. Then what is the Japanese system of morality, and how was it formed?"

I began searching for answers to these questions.

First, I read many books written by European philosophers, because Japanese people recently have been influenced by European culture. But I could find no answers to my questions.

Next, I read books that described the teachings of ancient Asian philosophers pre-dating Christ, such as Buddha, Confucius, and Lao-tze, with comments by famous Japanese professors of Asian culture. I knew that the Japanese system of morality is based on these teachings. I was especially impressed with a book entitled *Rongo (The Analects of Confucius)* by Dr. Shigeki Kaizuka, a noted professor of Chinese history at Kyoto University.

Based on his historical knowledge, Dr. Kaizuka explained the ideals of Confucius described in the Rongo. By reading Kaizuka's book intently, I recognized that Japanese morality and their view of life are based largely on the ideals of Confucius, a Chinese philosopher and educator (552-479 B.C.)

I began my own study by selecting sayings regarding morality from the *Analects of Confucius*. The sayings were not arranged in any particular order, so I grouped them into about fifty-five categories, putting related sayings in their own category. Then I classified these into seven sections. (A word processor was a very useful tool for arranging the sections.) My new arrangement showed clearly the system of morality that the Japanese people, for their mutual prosperity, had learned from Confucius.

As a company manager, I realized that Confucius' system of morality was most useful to me, but I had to know my wife's view. I explained my thoughts to my wife. Her view was that the Analects teach how we can prosper together and that housewives, too, could use them. I shared my thoughts with Sadakazu Shindo, the former chairman of Mitsubishi Electric, and he recommended that I write a book about the system.

Following Shindo's recommendation, I published a book in Japan that explains Confucius' system of morality and how it applies to the needs of modern businessmen. The book has been popular with not only managers and workers, but also housewives and students. This English edition is based on that Japanese book.

It is my purpose here to describe Confucian ideals for mutual prosperity that form the basis of Japanese business success.

I would like to thank Ms. Jackie Bonhaus of Mitsubishi Electric Manufacturing Cincinnati, in Ohio, who not only

2222

revised my manuscript, but also gave me valuable suggestions; Dr. T. Nakayama of Mitsubishi Electric Engineering Co., Ltd., and Dr. M. Ashkin of Westinghouse Electric Corporation, who gave me valuable advice regarding the translations of these sayings in the *Analects of Confucius;* Mr. Bill Totten, president of Ashisuto, who pointed out vague expressions from the American point of view; and Mr. Ric Fochtman, executive vice president of administration, Mitsubishi Electronics, America, Inc., who gave valued suggestions.

Confucius and the Japanese

Confucius was introduced more than a thousand years ago through the *Analects of Confucius.* The Analects, a collection of sayings by Confucius and his disciples, concern morality, manners, customs, and human relations. In the Edo period (1600-1867), the Shogunate family reigned in Japan under the concepts of Confucianism. Subsequently, the Analects were the main source of study for Japanese scholars and the main teaching material for schools. It was said that almost all intelligent people could recite the sayings in the Analects, while pupils of Teragoya, the primary schools in that era, could "recite the Analects without understanding them." ("Those who recite the Analects without understanding" is a popular idiom in Japan.)

Since Japan opened her doors to Western countries with the Meiji Restoration (1867-1912), the Analects have been studied in the context of their historical background by scholars of Chinese history and culture at Japanese universities, and many Japanese books on the Analects have been published. It is my opinion that the Analects have been studied more completely in Japan than in China or Korea, where the Analects have also been very popular.

Today, most Japanese know the Analects primarily as common sense ideas passed down through generations. Japanese people learn some of the Analects in their high school Chinese lessons. Following are some popular sayings that almost all Japanese people can recite:*

> He is a Gentleman who feels no discomposure when others fail to appreciate his competence.

> If one knows that his dream is realized in the morning, he is content, even if he dies in the same evening.

> Confucius said, "I started studying when a little older than fifteen. I knew my role as a scholar at thirty. I had consistency in my views at forty. I was conscious of the meaning of providence and human destiny at fifty. I was no longer argumentative at sixty. Now, at seventy, I do what I want but do not try to jump over my limits."

> Excess is as improper as lack.

> He is a coward who, fearing his superior's eyes, does not carry out a just act that his superior dislikes.

> Enjoying something is better than merely being interested in something. Being interested in something is better than merely knowing something.

> A Gentleman does not make himself into a mere machine fit only to do one kind of work.

> Not to reform oneself when one finds fault in oneself is to fail.

*Sayings and short stories taken from the Analects are shown in indented, non-justified form throughout this book.

In building an artificial mountain, if you abandon the task, even just before the last shovel of sand is heaped on it, you have failed.

To know what it is that you know and to know what it is that you do not know—that is knowledge.

How pleasant it is to learn and occasionally apply what we have learned.

Investigate established truths in detail and deduce new universal truths from them. Only those who can put this into practice can teach others.

A Gentleman behaves with harmony, objecting if he believes it necessary, while a vagrant does the opposite.

Good in one case may not be good in another.

Confucius did not forget loyalty and consideration for others throughout his life.

Do not force others to do what you do not want to do yourself.

You cannot play your proper role if you do not understand what polite manners are.

How pleasant it is to welcome friends who come from far away!

Do not befriend those who are unsuitable for you.

A Gentleman returns honesty for resentment, and virtue for virtue.

His will cannot be taken from the humblest man, while the captain-general can be taken even from the largest army.

The inferior manager will hope for too much when he employs a person.

It is impossible to make all of your employees understand all about management. But it is possible to make them work as you want.

To know a person, one must know his sayings.

Never set limits on the future of young persons. Their future can never be predicted from their present state.

Without a long-range plan, you will run into trouble in the short term.

Carry out a task after reviewing it twice. Three times is too often.

The world has changed a great deal since Confucius lived. Society has improved with advances in technology, and people know much more about nature and medicine thanks to advances in science. But morality has changed very little. This is why Confucian ideals are still alive in Japan. However, young people today are less able to recite the Analects because of the stress on science and technology in Japanese schools.

Confucian Thought

The World View of Confucius

Confucius, in his view of the world, stressed the importance of people's minds. This contrasts with modern scientific thought, which stresses substance and being in explaining the world. More precisely, Confucius viewed the world as a set of people mutually connected with complex linkages—so complex that no one can either forecast his own destiny or realize his own vision exactly as he intends. It seems that there is a supreme being (called *Ten* in Japanese) above us all that controls our destiny by a supreme control *(Mei* or *Tenmei)*. A popular saying from the Analects states:

> Death and life are determined by *Mei* and riches and honors depend upon *Ten*.

Confucius revealed his own view of the world when he was told that a statesman plotted to crush a political reform that Confucius had proposed:

It is *Mei* that determines whether my vision will be realized or not. What can a man do against *Mei*?

However, Confucius did not regard *Tenmei* as a direct control, like that of God. Confucius said,

What does *Ten* speak? The four seasons come around and every being is born and perishes, while *Ten* speaks nothing. What does *Ten* speak?

And he displayed no interest in gods and the supernatural, as his disciples said:

"Confucius never spoke of anomalies, rebellions, or divinities."

Replying to a question about how to serve the gods, Confucius said, "Keep away from the gods, while respecting them, and devote yourself to general justice and law."

Replying to a question about the help of gods for healing sickness, Confucius said, "I have never prayed for the gods to heal my sickness."

Likewise, Confucius showed little interest in the world after death.

Replying to a question about death, Confucius said, "I do not understand life. How can I understand death?"

Confucius thought that human society was formed, not by gods, but by evolution.

Human society has evolved day and night without a pause, involving everyone. It is as if a big river flows.

It is interesting to note that Confucius thought that his ideas were too advanced to be understood by contemporary people and complained to Tze Kung, his wisest disciple.

"No one understands me," Confucius complained. Tze Kung responded, "Why did you say that so abruptly?" Confucius said, "I do not resent *Ten* or blame people. But only *Ten* knows that I have studied practical things around us diversely and comprehend the profound truth underneath them."

The Jin of Confucius

The most fundamental concept Confucius gave is called *Jin* in Japanese. According to Confucius, there are not only right linkages, which help people to prosper, but also wrong linkages, which cause society to decline. *Jin* stands for those deeds that induce the right linkages. Conventionally, it is translated into English as "true virtue," but its meaning is actually far broader than the term indicates. I will, therefore, use the Japanese word *Jin* without translation. Remember that the Analects describe the discussions of Confucius and his disciples regarding what deeds work for or against *Jin*.

Confucius thought that *Jin* was indispensable to the survival of people, and said,

Human beings need *Jin* far more than water and fire.

Confucius thought further that it was due to *Jin* that human society has evolved successfully.

> Human society has evolved successfully because human beings have accepted *Jin* sincerely.

> In the evolution, those who did not accept *Jin* eventually perished, although they sometimes survived for a while accidentally.

> No one is disliked so long as he lives according to *Jin*.

Confucius explained the principles of *Jin* concisely with the following sayings:

> *Jin* is to love one another.

> *Jin* is the loyalty to and the consideration of others.

> The foundation of *Jin* is that all members of a family live in harmony.

> *Jin* is respect, generosity, prudence, fidelity, quickness, and kindness.

> Quickness belongs to *Jin*, because a quick accomplishment results in a prominent result.

To practice *Jin*, Confucius advised as follows:

> *Jin* is not a remote ideal; if we try to seek it, then it comes near.

> The practice of *Jin* is dependent solely on one's will; it is not dependent on others.

> When practicing *Jin*, one should defer to no one, not even to his teacher.

As to the method of the practice, Confucius thought:

> Shunning those who violate *Jin* is one of the ways to practice *Jin*.

> Practice *Jin* in daily life whenever necessary. Then you will gradually master *Jin*.

> Anyone can practice *Jin* if he makes up his mind to do so with all his might at least this one day.

Confucius must have wanted to say further, "Then one can practice it likewise the next day and so on. Thus one can practice it every day."

The Master of Jin

Confucius regarded mastery of *Jin* in its entirety as the ultimate goal of human beings, as the following saying shows.

> Those who have aspired and attained the mastery of *Jin* need nothing more.

According to Confucius, the Master of *Jin*, he who can practice *Jin* unconsciously so that he never violates it is an ideal person. It should be pointed out that mastering *Jin* is an ideal and that Confucius neither called himself the Master of *Jin* nor allowed others to call him so. What, then, is the Master of *Jin*? Confucius defined the Wise Person to make it easier to describe the Master. The Wise Person, according to Confucius, is an intelligent person who is not yet aware of *Jin* in its entirety and makes full use of his high intelligence and partial understanding of *Jin* to acquire money, things, and honor. But he never acquires satisfaction. Needless to say, Confucius thought more highly of the Master of *Jin* than of the Wise Person.

If he cannot yet be said to be a Wise Person, how can he be a Master of *Jin*?

He defined a Master of *Jin* sometimes by comparing him with a Wise Person, as in the following:

The Master of *Jin* relies upon *Jin* while the Wise Person only decorates himself with *Jin*.

The Master of *Jin* is a person who finds beauty in deeds according to *Jin*.

The Master of *Jin* has no anxiety, while the Wise Person has no confusions but sometimes has anxiety.

The Master of *Jin* is calm and takes delight in the serenity of mountains, while the Wise Person is restless and takes delight in the active flow of rivers.

The Master of *Jin* enjoys long life while the Wise Person enjoys each moment.

It is only the Master of *Jin* who can like and dislike others correctly.

Those who are tough spiritually and prudent in speech are approaching a Master of *Jin*.

The Master of *Jin* is not a smooth talker. Generally, it is very difficult to do exactly what one has promised to do. How can the Master of *Jin* be a smooth talker?

A talkative and flattering person has little of *Jin*.

Confucius must have wanted to say that the Wise Person wants to speak too much.

Moreover, Confucius thought that possessing bravery is essential to the mastering of *Jin*.

The Master of *Jin* is a brave person, but not vice versa.

The Follower of Jin

Followers of *Jin* are eager to learn *Jin*; they strive to spread *Jin* among people for the prosperity of society. In other words, followers of *Jin* are those who work to become a Master of *Jin*. It should be pointed out that the phrase "follower of *Jin*" shares attributes, to some extent, with the word "gentleman" in English, although it is not related to the idea of "family background." Therefore, I will refer to the "follower of *Jin*" as a "Gentleman" in the text. Please note as well that, although gentleman usually refers to the male gender, my use, to connote "follower of *Jin*," applies to any person, male or female.

As for a Gentleman, Confucius explained:

> A Gentleman never forgets *Jin* for a moment, even while eating, even while "tumbling."

> A Gentleman plays his role after learning *Jin* sufficiently.

> Since a Gentleman learns *Jin* sufficiently, he respects everybody and makes any person feel confident and comfortable when the person works with him.

> He is not a Gentleman who does not understand the meaning *Mei*.

Besides, Confucius put more value on spiritual matters and dissuaded a Gentleman from seeking an extravagant life. He said,

I do not call him a Gentleman who is ashamed of his humble clothes and food, however earnestly he strives to learn *Jin.*

A person who is concerned with a comfortable dwelling is not a Gentleman, even if he calls himself so.

Please note that Confucius thought the primary object of politics is to improve not only spiritual but physical structure of society.

A disciple asked, "What should I do first as a statesman?" Confucius replied, "Enrich your state first, then think how to educate your people."

I worry that the Japanese today put too much value on seeking an extravagant life.

Confucius' Principle of Education

As a state official, Confucius thought that the opportunity for education should not depend on wealth or social class. In other words, he thought that everyone had the right to learn. He said:

The opportunity for education should be freed from restrictions of social class.

As an educator, the first traveling teacher, Confucius thought that, unless people learned positively with excitement, a teacher could not educate them.

It is nonsense to teach anyone except he who is stimulated by the joy of learning. It will be in vain to teach anyone except he who is willing to prepare his lessons sufficiently. I drop such a lazy pupil who fails to try to figure out the other three corners after being told of one corner of a four-sided figure.

A teacher can instruct nobody except he who asks persistently how to deal with this, what is the meaning of that, and so on.

It is a well-known fact that this principle of education raised the standard of education in Japan during the nineteenth century to such an extent that by the end of the century Japan's literacy rate ranked highest in the world. Owing to this high standard of education, Japan was able to industrialize about one hundred years ago, at the end of the nineteenth century, almost the same time as European countries.

Moreover, a former prime minister of Singapore said that this Confucian principle of education enabled his young nation to raise its standard of education and so to industrialize. I think this is true of all of Asia's newly industrialized economies in which the morality of the people is based on the teachings of Confucius.

Dreams of Confucius

One of the dreams of Confucius was to realize a society in which people filed no lawsuits. Confucius thought that if all people have consideration of others they would not file lawsuits. He said,

I can handle a lawsuit well if I become a judge. However, it is my dream to make a society in which there are no lawsuits.

Another dream was a country where all people respected older persons. This idea is particularly important for the Japanese because the average life span there is the highest in the world. Confucius said,

> I want to make a society in which aged persons can feel easy and assured.

His final dream was to enjoy his leisure time, as the following story shows:

> Confucius agreed with Tseng Tien, his eldest disciple, who said, "I like to imagine as follows: On a fine holiday in early summer, I go on a hike with five or six of my men, accompanied by their children, all wearing new clothes just tailored in this late spring. On the hike we stop to bathe in the Ki River, have our lunches in the open-air theater, and cool ourselves in the pleasant breeze. Finally, we go home singing many songs.

It is a great surprise that these dreams, which Confucius had more than two thousand years ago, are still relevant today. This shows that the essence of human nature has not changed, despite the progress of science and technology.

Confucian Ideals for the Japanese

LEADING LIFE

Important Sayings

If we know that our dreams have been realized in the morning, we will be content, even if we die in the same evening.

A person establishes his principles independent of others; therefore, it is rare that a principle becomes an official doctrine accepted by the general population.

A person who is concerned with a comfortable dwelling in his native place is not a Gentleman, even if he calls himself so.

First consider what you can do, and then think of remuneration.

A Gentleman serves a superior only if the superior esteems the Gentleman's vision and principles, otherwise he quits.

Enjoying something is better than merely being interested in something. Being interested in something is better than merely knowing something.

A Gentleman pursues his own dream or objective earnestly, not competing with anyone.

He is a Gentleman who feels no discomposure when others fail to appreciate his competence.

The person who lacks confidence can do nothing useful. How can a cart move if its wheels have no axle or its horse has no harness?

A coward cannot maintain consistency. He is a coward who, fearing his superior's eyes, does not carry out a just act that his superior dislikes.

Lead a Significant Life

Live to pursue your dream.

Confucius said, "If we know that our dreams have been realized in the morning, we will be content even if we die in the same evening."

Have your own dream independent of others.

Confucius said, "It is rare for two persons graduating from the same school at the same time to pursue the same dream or objective."

Confucius said, "A person establishes his principles independent of others; therefore, it is rare that a principle becomes an official doctrine accepted by the general population."

According to Confucius, the basic condition of mutual prosperity is to enjoy freedom in which everybody can live a life of self-realization. Confucius predicted the collapse of the Soviet Union.

Do not mind leaving your native place for your dream.

> Confucius went abroad from age fifty-six to seventy in order to realize his political dream, which had been denied in his native country. On the journey he took his closest disciple with him. Confucius persuaded the disciples to go abroad with him, saying, "A person who is concerned with a comfortable dwelling in his native place is not a Gentleman, even if he calls himself so. A person without his own sure vision is always concerned only about his native place. He is never a Gentleman. In whatever place a Gentleman lives, that is the best place for him to live."

In the era during which Confucius lived, there were quite a number of independent countries in China. This was a war-torn period when people traveling between these countries must have felt at high risk and suffered great inconvenience. There were no passports, and the great distances were covered by simple means of transportation. Though these journeys were "regional" (rather than journeys abroad, as we would term them today), readiness of mind was a requirement of travel.

Do Not Distort Your Dream Easily

Do not violate your principles to earn quick money.

> Confucius said, "Everyone wants money or a high position. However, if one obtains money or position, deviating from his career planned on the basis of his principles, then he will lose both sooner or later."

> Confucius taught his disciples who were going to take jobs: "First consider what you can do, and then think of the remuneration."

> Confucius said, "A Gentleman thinks of his principle first, while a mean person is always concerned with profit."

It would be interesting to know Confucius' opinion about today's graduates, who prefer to take their first jobs in service industries only because the starting salaries are higher.

Quit your company if it forces you to violate your principles.

> Confucius said, "A Gentleman serves a king who administers his country with justice, otherwise he quits his job."

> Confucius said, "A Gentleman serves his superior only if the superior esteems the Gentleman's vision and principles, otherwise he quits."

> In old China, there was a statesman, Kuan Chung, whose superior was killed by his own brother. Later, Kuan Chung received an important post under the brother, placing in question Kuan Chung's loyalty to his former superior. Confucius' bravest disciple, Tze Lu, asked Confucius if Kuan Chung was virtuous or not. Confucius

32

replied, "He assisted his monarch in efforts to unify all Chinese countries by peaceful persuasion and without the force of war. People have received many benefits from their efforts. He was a great man of virtue, was he not?"

That the above saying and story are popular in Japan today may imply that the contemporary Japanese's loyalty to his company is a temporary phenomenon.

Enjoy Your Life, Forget Sorrows

Enjoy everything, even your job.

> Confucius said, "Enjoying something is better than merely being interested in something. Being interested in something is better than merely knowing something."

> Confucius enjoyed even working.

In today's highly pressured world, we all must work to earn a living; for many it seems difficult to enjoy their jobs. However, if we carry out our work seriously, we can become interested in the work, and soon become absorbed in it. This absorption allows us not only to forget difficulties in our lives, but can bring us delight in our good achievements.

Forget sorrows by being absorbed in work.

> Confucius often forgot to take meals in his effort to overcome difficulty in acquiring knowledge; consequently he forgot the sorrowful events in his life. Thus absorbed, he did not notice that old age was stealing up on him.

Have at least one hobby.

> Someone asked Confucius of his most favorite hobby. Confucius responded jokingly, "What is my most favorite hobby? Is it horse riding or shooting?"
>
> Confucius listened to music during his stay abroad. His impressions were so strong that for three months he could not taste meat, his favorite dish. He said, "I had not known that the impression of good music was so great."
>
> When Confucius listened to a good song, he asked the singer to repeat it until he could sing it himself.

Confucius was a prominent rider as well as a famous shooter. He was particularly fond of music.

Take useful pleasures, but not wrong ones.

> Confucius said, "There are three useful pleasures: to have many good friends, to enjoy music moderately, and to talk of the merits of others."
>
> Confucius said, "There are three wrong pleasures: to live in extravagance, to eat and drink luxuriously, and to be lecherous."

Confucius, whom people regarded as a sage, had many hobbies and took every spare moment to enjoy them, shunning wrong pleasures. Hobbies are indispensable means for driving human lives.

Avoid Meaningless Competition

Pursue your ideals, but don't compete meaninglessly.

> Confucius said, "A Gentleman pursues his own dream or objective earnestly without competing with anyone."

Compete to train yourself.

> Confucius explained to a respected senior for his agreement: "A Gentleman never competes in anything, except in archery. Even in archery, they do not compete in the skill of the game measured by the number of arrows that hit the target, because there are differences in gifted ability to hit the target. Instead, they compete in excellence of manner in which the game is played. To be more specific, they shoot arrows from a stand with stairs. When ascending and descending the stairs, they give way to each other. Then they pour wine in each other's cup and drink it. Thus, they play the archery game in order to build their characters and manners."

Competition is unavoidable in free society and contributes to the society's evolution. In competing with others, however, we should concentrate on attaining our goals or training ourselves rather than simply defeating another person. Regrettably, too many people today consider defeating others as the sole aim in competition; they are more concerned with winning games than enjoying them.

Do Not Lose Composure

Always keep perfect composure.

> Confucius said, "A Gentleman lives his long cherished
> dream keeping composure, while a vagrant chases after
> trivial things, always feeling irritation."

> Confucius remonstrated with a young disciple: "Be careful
> of losing your sense in a sudden fit of anger. It may involve
> your family."

Do not worry if you can believe in yourself.

> A disciple of Confucius, whose brother had tormented
> Confucius and the other disciples, said that he might not
> be able to become a Gentleman because of his brother's
> wrong doings. Confucius responded, "Neither feel worry
> nor fear if your self-examination reveals nothing wrong in
> yourself."

> Confucius said, "A Gentleman considers his own
> weakness without considering if others have
> underestimated him."

> Confucius said, "A Gentleman considers his inability to
> serve a certain post, but does not worry about being given
> the high position."

> Confucius said, "A Gentleman always considers whether
> his estimations of others are right or not, remaining
> unconcerned with others' estimation of him."

Strive to get prominent results when ignored.

> Confucius said, "A Gentleman does not worry about being recognized; rather he strives to do great things that are recognized by all."

An adversity is one of the best opportunities by which a Gentleman can improve his ability.

Strive to Earn Trust Based on Consistency

Earn trust before everything by maintaining consistency.

> Confucius said, "The person who lacks confidence cannot do anything useful. How can a cart move if its wheels have no axle or its horse has no harness?"

> Confucius said, "Without consistency, you lose trust. Then you cannot get a proper job that requires trust, such as a prophetess or a doctor."

Japanese people, when changing their minds, often excuse themselves by reciting a non-Confucian saying: "A Gentleman improves his thinking as quickly as a leopard changes its spots." (People of the Far East believe that a leopard can quickly conform its coloration to new surroundings.)

Learn what behavior causes inconsistency.

> Confucius said, "We are said to be independent and consistent if we do not change our causes, which we have stated to others for so long."

Confucius said, "If our consistency is not based on virtue, then we will lose it and incur disgrace sooner or later."

Confucius said, "A coward cannot be consistent. He is a coward who, fearing his superior's eyes, does not carry out a just act that his superior dislikes."

Confucius said, "If one pretends to be rich or to have precious things or knowledge, then sooner or later he will show inconsistency."

Confucius said, "Who calls Wei-shen Kao honest? When someone asked for vinegar, he sought it from a neighbor and gave it to the person without explanation. Wei-shen Kao must be called dishonest."

WORKING

Important Sayings

A Gentleman does not make himself into a machine fit only for one kind of work.

In natural gifts, we are close to each other; it is the effort to learn that separates us.

An idiot does not become a highly intelligent person, or vice versa.

A Gentleman allows his fault to be as evident as an eclipse, while a vagrant hides his fault. And everyone admires the Gentleman when he makes amends.

Not to reform oneself when one finds fault in oneself is to fail.

Excess is as improper as lack.

A Gentleman does not join hands with a reckless person who fights against a wild tiger with his bare hands or crosses a rapid stream on foot in winter.

A Gentleman does everything to respond to the urgent demands of a person in true need, but pays no heed to the redundant demands of a rich man.

In the building of an artificial mountain, for example, if you abandon the task even just before the last shovel of sand is heaped onto it you have failed.

Develop your ability systematically

Plan your career by referring to Confucius.

> Confucius said, "I started studying when a little older than fifteen. I knew my role as a scholar at thirty. I had consistency in my views at forty. I was conscious of the meaning of *Mei* at fifty. I was no longer argumentative at sixty. Now, at seventy, I do what I want but do not try to jump past my limits."
>
> Confucius taught his disciple regarding career development, "Do not be hasty by wanting only quick progress."

To begin one's studies after the age of fifteen seems late, but other careers are still relevant today, while our average life span is much longer.

Be a specialist during your youth.

> Confucius mastered many things from his youth. Therefore, he was asked by several whether one had to master many things or not when young. Confucius answered, "I was forced to master many things in my youth because I was too obscure to have a fixed job. Should a young Gentleman with a fixed or promised job try to master many things in his youth? Never."

Mastering a specialty in one's youth enables one to gain sure knowledge and thus take broad responsibilities in later life.

Be a generalist in middle age.

> Confucius said, "A Gentleman does not make himself into a mere machine fit for only one kind of work."

> Confucius was pleased with the following comment of an official: "Confucius is great. He has mastered so many things that we cannot tell what his specialty is."

The current period of time is referred to by some as the "age of specialty." There are many specialists who refuse to broaden their expertise beyond their specialties. I am afraid this will produce a scarcity of leaders in the near future.

Recognize the importance of both effort and talent

Recognize the importance of effort.

> Confucius said, "In natural gifts, we are close to each other; it is the effort to learn that separates us."

> Confucius said, "There are inferior seeds that cannot grow up to become trees. However, there are many superior seeds that can grow up to become trees, but will bear no fruit because of no effort in later life."

> Confucius reflected upon his life in his later years and said, "I was not born a genius. Since I learned history with much effort, I was able to become an expert."

> Confucius scolded his lazy disciple: "I do not carve rotten wood. I do not repair walls made from the droppings of animals. A person who does not extend an effort is like rotten wood or walls made from droppings."

The willingness to study and work hard is, in itself, a valuable talent. But beyond this, willingness is the talent that distinguishes great people from their peers.

Make the best use of talent.

> Confucius said, "An idiot does not become a highly intelligent person, or vice versa."

> Confucius said, "A genius who has a gifted talent is the highest; a person who makes himself knowledgeable by learning voluntarily before meeting difficulties is the second highest, and a person who learns in order to solve only the difficulties at hand is the third."

Someone from the Republic of China once criticized Confucius for discriminating against people because of their natural gifts. I agree with Confucius for the reason that each of us has different talents; if we attempt to find work that fits our talents and strive to excel anybody can become great.

Make failure a stepping stone to success

Do not lose composure even when you find a serious mistake.

> From the age of fifty-six to seventy, Confucius traveled abroad with his disciples. They were involved in a war and lost their food supply because of a mistaken decision on Confucius' part to start on a certain date. Tze Lu, the closest disciple, blamed Confucius for the failure, and asked, "Does it happen that a Gentleman falls into serious trouble?" Confucius replied, "Of course he does. But it is a vagrant who loses his composure when in trouble."

Confucius said, "I am happy to have many friends who confide my mistakes as soon as I commit them."

We should not be ashamed of failure. Even a person as great as Confucius sometimes failed and fell into trouble because of his failure. However, Confucius used every failure for later success. For him, every failure was a stepping stone to success.

Do not hide mistakes.

> Tze Kung, the clever disciple, said, "A Gentleman allows his mistakes to be as evident as an eclipse, while a vagrant hides his fault. And everyone admires the Gentleman when he makes amends."
>
> Confucius said, "A Gentleman accepts his complete responsibility for failure in himself while a vagrant seeks it in others."

We see too many employers today who get angry when subordinates point out their employers' faults. These employers must commit the same faults again.

Strive not to commit the same failure twice.

> Confucius said, "Not to reform oneself when one finds fault in oneself is to make a failure."
>
> Confucius told his disciple, "Do not be reluctant to make reforms when you find fault in yourself. Note that there are few who blame themselves when they recognize their faults.

Have several checkpoints for your behavior

Check your performance at every opportunity.

Confucius said, "I check my performance according to nine checkpoints associated with the following nine actions:

1. when listening, understand well
2. when acting, see clearly
3. when looking at others, show a warm heart
4. when facing others, show humility
5. when talking, be truthful
6. when performing a deed, be prudent
7. when doubting, ask
8. when feeling anger, fear consequences
9. when making profits, be just."

Change your checkpoints depending upon age.

Confucius said, " A Gentleman should change his checkpoints three times, depending upon his age, as follows: When he is young, he is hot-blooded, so he should check his tender passion. When he is in his middle years, he is firmly self-confident, so he should check his fighting spirit. When he is old, he has little will to perform by himself, so he should check his propensity to dependence."

Never be excessive

Be moderate rather than excessive.

> Tze Kung, the talkative disciple, asked Confucius, "Who is superior, Mr. A or Mr. B?" Confucius replied, "Mr. A is too wise and Mr. B is not so wise." Tze Kung asked further, "Then is Mr. A superior to Mr. B?" Confucius replied, "Excess is as improper as lack."

> Confucius taught his aggressive disciple: "Be moderate so that you are not likely to lose your health and wealth."

Take the middle of the road.

> Confucius said, "The merit of the middle of the road is superior."

While the Japanese economy was growing rapidly between the 1950s and the 1970s, many businessmen and their employees worked like beavers, devoting themselves so intensely to their jobs that they neglected their families (not only parents, but wives and children as well). This, of course, brought on many complaints from the families, which worried the businessmen. During the past decade, however, the number of workers and employers who work excessively has declined significantly.

Select a person with whom to cooperate or aid

Do not join hands with a reckless man.

> Confucius said to Yen Hui, the virtuous disciple, "I can
> join hands with you in everything." Tze Lu, the brave but
> hasty disciple, who heard this, said, "You should join
> hands with me in a war." Confucius responded, "A
> Gentleman does not join hands with a reckless person
> who fights against a wild tiger with his bare hands or
> crosses a rapid stream on foot in winter. Those with whom
> the Gentleman works are prudent persons who like
> planning."

To "avoid braveness like wrestling a wild tiger or crossing a
rapid stream on foot" is a popular Japanese expression.

Do not respond to a rich person's redundant demands.

> Confucius said, "A Gentleman does everything to respond
> to the urgent demands of a person in true need, but pays
> no heed to the redundant demands of a rich man."

Know that people with different objectives do not cooperate.

> Confucius said, "Two men whose principles differ seldom
> cooperate."

Perform a task step by step, seriously and actively

Take a piece and the finish of a work seriously.

> Confucius said, "In the building of an artificial mountain, if you abandon the task, even just before the last shovel of sand is heaped on it, you have failed. In the construction of a road, you make progress when you heap even one shovel of earth."

Some of today's university graduates want to heap too many shovels of earth at a time. According to Confucius, these people will find it difficult to succeed.

Carry out the most difficult task first.

> Confucius said, "The Master of *Jin* executes the difficult things first and then the easy things, which he knows he can do."

People are apt to do the easiest thing first, wanting a quicker advance in their tasks.

Employ others without reserve when performing a task.

> To control his aggressiveness, Tze Lu, the bravest disciple, recited daily the following saying in a poem: "So long as one does no harm and requires nothing, he will do nothing wrong." Confucius commented, "That is too passive to be achieved."

Do not begrudge doing anything.

> Confucius said, "He is the worst kind of person who does
> nothing except fool around throughout the day,
> begrudging that his work is troublesome. I have heard that
> there is a rogue who is called a Gambler. Such an idle
> person is worse than the Gambler."

Confucius considered idleness the mother of all evil.

LEARNING

Important Sayings

> To know what it is that you know, and to know what it is that you do not know—that is knowledge.

> Deliberation without learning brings dogmatism. Learning without deliberation results only in obscure knowledge.

> How pleasant it is to learn and occasionally apply what we have learned.

> Never tire of learning. Learn new things everyday and try to remember them every month.

> Study hard throughout your life, no matter how rich or poor you are, in the same way that an artisan tirelessly cuts and polishes a precious stone.

> When we work together with three persons, we are taught by at least one of them. When we see a wise person, we give thought to attaining his stature. When we see an unwise person, we reflect upon our own actions.

> Do not feel any shame in asking questions of your subordinates.

> To use unorthodox texts for your learning is only harmful.

> Investigate established truths in detail and deduce new universal truths from them. Only those who put this into practice can teach others and be called experts.

> Those who can neither administer a country nor go on a mission abroad are not great, even if they can recite three hundred poems.

Study poetry. Poetry cultivates common sense, teaches you subjects of interest and the views of common people, and how to cooperate.

Understand the object and purpose of learning

Know what knowledge is before you learn.

Confucius remonstrated with Tze Lu (who sometimes pretended to know): "To know what it is that you know and to know what it is that you do not know—that is knowledge."

Enjoy learning.

Confucius said, "How pleasant it is to learn and occasionally apply what we have learned."

Know the evil affects of disliking learning.

Confucius said, "Deliberation without learning brings dogmatism."

Confucius taught Tze Lu, who was too practical: "Foolishness results if you like *Jin* but dislike learning. Incoherence results if you like intelligence but dislike learning. Naïveté results if you like confidence but dislike learning. Stubbornness results if you like honesty but dislike learning. Rebelliousness results if you like bravery but dislike learning. Madness results if you like power but dislike learning.

You must study adequately before you can lead people.

> Tze Hsia, the disciple who was a writer, wrote: "A superior artisan produces good work after first constructing a good workplace. Likewise, a Gentleman performs best after first establishing an excellent knowledge base."

Study hard and tirelessly throughout life

Always study hard and tirelessly.

> Confucius taught his disciples, "Study hard, thinking always that you lack the proper eagerness to study. Review often, fearing to forget what you have learned."

> And again, Confucius taught: "Never tire of learning. Learn new things everyday and try to remember them every month."

Study urgent problems, referring to phenomena at hand.

> Tze Hsia wrote, "Learn many things earnestly and establish your ambition firmly. Then study urgent problems referring to phenomena at hand. Thus, you can gradually approach the complete understanding of *Jin*."

Learn throughout life.

> Confucius said, "To learn even after fifty is indispensable if you want to be free from major errors."

> Confucius loved the following saying from a famous

poem: "Study hard throughout your life, as an artisan tirelessly cuts and polishes a precious stone, no matter how rich or how poor you are."

The amount of knowledge to learn accumulates yearly: knowledge of humanity, politics, economics, science and technology, and so on. The need to keep up learning, therefore, is much greater today than in the time of Confucius.

You cannot continue to learn if you learn only to earn fame.

> Confucius said, "Great scholars in the past learned to enlighten themselves, so they continued to learn. Today's scholars learn in order to achieve fame, so they stop learning when they finally achieve it."

If we learn in order to cultivate ourselves, then we eagerly continue to learn throughout life. But if we learn only in order to gain fame or please our families, then we lose our eagerness to learn when we have attained such a small goal.

Learn from every person

First learn from teachers and superiors.

> Tze Hsia wrote, "Adore a wise person as ardently as you love a beauty."

> Confucius said, "A great craftsman sharpens his tools before he produces good work. Likewise, a Gentleman cultivates his character through learning about *Jin* from a wise manager by serving him and from good friends by associating with them before he performs as a leader."

Confucius said, "A sleepless night throughout which I thought by myself in vain showed me the need of learning from wise persons."

Confucius said, "One cannot understand the essence of humanity without following seniors who have gone ahead."

It is certain that we become more knowledgeable over time. This is not because the physical body of our brain has increased but because we use more knowledge accumulated in society. Our teachers and elders share this accumulation. Therefore it is far more effective to learn first from the experience of our teachers and elders than to try to reason by ourselves and rely only upon texts.

Try to learn from inferiors.

Recalling Yen Hui, the senior disciple who was loved by Confucius and died in his youth, Tsang, the successor to Confucius as a scholar, said, "Using his higher ability, he learned something from the less competent. He tried to make progress by listening to those who have made less progress."

Confucius praised a statesman who did not feel any shame in asking questions of his subordinates.

Try to learn also from unwise persons.

Confucius said, "When I work together with three persons, I am taught by at least one of them. When I see a wise person, I give thought to attaining his stature. When I see an unwise person, I reflect upon my own actions."

The Japanese have a popular idiom about learning from bad examples. In fact, the wrongful deeds of an unwise person are sometimes a more effective teacher than the good deeds of a wise person.

Select good sources

Use only authentic sources.

> Confucius said, "To use unorthodox texts for your learning is only harmful."
>
> Tze Hsia wrote: "Even unimportant learning contains something interesting. But note that to study such things too earnestly can hamper one's important learning."

We have so many things to master in our life that we have little time to share the unimportant things; life is short, while art is long.

Learn about humanity from novels and poems.

> Confucius recommended that we study poetry: "Study poetry—poems cultivate common sense, teach you subjects of interest and the views of common people, and how to cooperate with one another, as well as the names of birds, beasts, grasses, and trees."
>
> In teaching, Confucius was fair to all his students. He did not treat even his own son specially. The only thing he taught his son specially was the importance of learning poems. Whenever Confucius met his son he said, "Are

you learning poems? Otherwise, you cannot learn speaking ability."

It is one of the serious problems today that engineers are so busy learning new technologies they do not have time to learn the literary works, such as poetry or novels. I am afraid they will lack the culture required of a Gentleman.

Think out new ideas from knowledge obtained

In contemplation, digest what you have already learned.

> Confucius said, "Learning without contemplation results only in obscure knowledge."
>
> Confucius said, "What I did was to digest knowledge by contemplation until it became my own and I never tired of studying."

We can think extensively from a broad viewpoint if we contemplate problems in a dark room or by closing our eyes. It is recommended that we contemplate problems by meditation. Besides, meditation makes it possible to think almost anywhere at almost any given opportunity (for example, when in bed or while on an airplane or even when driving a car). Meditation, thus, makes us think throughout the day.

Deep contemplation enables us to think as in dreams.

> Old Confucius said, "It is regrettable that my thinking power became too weak to see the Great Duke of Chou in my dreams."

Deep meditation makes us think as in a dream. Confucius' regret shows that his deep meditation often induced dreams when he studied on a great king of Chou.

Find new universal facts from past facts.

> Confucius said, "Investigate established truths in detail and deduce new universal truths from them. Only those who can put this into practice can teach others or be called experts."

> Confucius taught his disciple, who was a scholar, "Examine as many established truths as possible at first, then remember only those that are useful for your study. Observe as many facts as possible with your own eyes and memorize only those that are effective for your study. Then put them in order, and then in another order. Repeat this process again and again by deep contemplation. Thus, you can gradually approach new universal truths."

> Confucius said, "In the study of human relations, it is especially useful to categorize the facts according to social order."

These popular sayings explain Confucius' method of study. While science seeks to discover universal laws, Confucius sought to discover universal truths. Even today, Confucius' method is used by humanities scholars who use phenomenology to study philosophy.

Study and work

Study through on-the-job training.

> Tze Lu, the practical disciple, said, "We have many examples to learn, at the office as well as in the field. Why should we have a job only after learning with many books?"

> Confucius said, "Study *Jin* by making use of the examples around you."

Confucius recommended on-the-job training here.

Practice what you have learned.

> Tze Lu said, "I do not want to learn new things until I have practiced everything I have learned."

Apply your study to practical matters.

> Confucius said, "Those who can neither administer a country nor go on a mission abroad are not great, even if they can recite three hundred poems."

> Comparing the knowledge of Confucius to a gem, Tze Kung said, "There is a beautiful gem here. Should we keep it safe or should we seek a good price and sell it?" Confucius said, "Let's sell it. Sell it. We should look for someone who will offer a good price."

> A notorious statesman asked Confucius to be his consultant. Confucius was going to accept. Tze Lu was

opposed, and said to Confucius, "Do not accept it. You said that you never cooperate with those who act wrongly. This statesman has plundered the land of his superior by making use of a poor stratagem. Does your action contradict what you said?" Confucius answered, "Yes, I said so. However, I have changed my mind because I have recently become a truly hard and white stone, as in the following maxim: 'If it is truly hard, we cannot make it thin and pliable, however much one polishes it, however much one oils it.' I am not jobless. How can I continue to be a bitter cucumber that hangs down a branch without notice?"

Speaking

Important Sayings

A Gentleman behaves with harmony, but objects if he believes it is necessary; a vagrant does the opposite.

Be certain of the feasibility of your own acts before you say you will do or recommend something.

A Gentleman feels a strong sense of shame when he boasts.

Everyone will have to pay attention to you if you talk at the right time.

A Gentleman does not evaluate someone only by his words; neither does a Gentleman reject the words of someone who is underestimated.

A good businessman comprehends what a person wants to say, not only by his words but by his eyes.

Be earnest in advising friends. But as soon as you feel their disgust, stop the advice.

Do not talk persistently about past matters. Do not remonstrate on deeds already done. Do not find blame for errors already committed.

Do not pass on what you have heard before first grasping its essence.

Those who secretly attack the character or deeds of others should be shunned.

Speak positively, but carefully

Speak your opinion.

> Confucius said, "You will be thought a tricky person hiding something if you do not speak out when you should."
>
> Confucius said, "A virtuous person speaks his opinion positively."
>
> Confucius said, "You will lose your friends if you do not talk to them when you should."

We should state our opinion if we want to associate with others on a friendly basis. Otherwise, not only will we be misunderstood, but we may become disliked or disdained by others, as an unfriendly person.

The Japanese says "no" to object to what someone asks, while the English say "no" to deny the verb in the question. As is well known, Japanese people avoid saying "no" in conversation, even if they believe "no" is appropriate; they fear that "no" would break harmony. But they are wrong. If one believes that "no" is the proper response, one should dare to say "no."

State objections if you believe they are necessary.

> Confucius said, "A Gentleman behaves with harmony, but makes objections if he believes necessary, while a vagrant does the opposite."

Smooth relations cannot be kept with associates unless opinions are expressed clearly, even if these opinions are objections. If colleagues hold back objections, thinking that silence is wisdom, then the frustration they have accumulated will make

60

them backbite their associates so that the harmonious association eventually will be broken.

State positively the good deeds of people.

> Confucius said, "It is useful to talk well of the good deeds of others."

Speak carefully.

> Tze Kung, the clever disciple, said, "A Gentleman is observed by many; just one of his words can lead to an evaluation of him, whether he is wise or not. Therefore, a Gentleman must speak prudently."

> Confucius said, "Words on everyone's tongue go faster than a carriage and four."

Speak honestly, but try to go beyond your words

Do not say what you are uncertain about.

> Tze Kung asked about a Gentleman. Confucius answered, "A Gentleman makes sure of the feasibility of his own acts before he says that he will do or recommend something."

In general, today's managers make attractive speeches. They refine their speeches, making full use of the so-called "presentation technique" and lots of rehearsal. However, it sometimes happens that these managers decorate their speeches with words that are unconfirmed and thoughts that are not feasible; they try to sell themselves too much by their speech.

Try to go beyond what you have promised.

> Confucius said, "It is a person of small scale who always acts only within his words, but never beyond his words."

Feel shame when you boast.

> A Gentleman feels a strong sense of shame when he boasts.

> "It is difficult to achieve what one says if one cannot imagine the shame of failing to do so."

Though most people are tempted to talk at every opportunity, we should be careful not to be too talkative. We must be responsible for what we say. We should understand that, in general, there is a great difference between words and deeds.

Never be a glib speaker.

> Confucius said, "Controlling others with smooth talk only violates the principles of virtue."

> A lord who had hired a disciple of Confucius spoke ill of that disciple: "He understands *Jin* quite well, but is a poor speaker." Confucius argued to the lord, "Controlling others with fluent words often leads only to being disliked."

Strive to make the best use of dialogue

Select a person to talk to.

> Confucius said, "If you talk to an unworthy person, you will waste your time; if you do not talk with a worthy person, you will lose good friendship."

Comprehend what others say also from their faces.

> Confucius said, "You are said to be blind if you talk without watching the eyes of the person you talk to."
>
> "A good businessman comprehends what a person wants to say, not only by words but also by his eyes."

Never give bad impressions to others.

> Tsang said, "Beware of rudeness when you are looking at others. Beware of savagery when you are speaking."
>
> A man explained to Confucius why a famous statesman was loved by people: "He laughs only when he feels real pleasure, therefore nobody shows displeasure. He speaks only when he should, therefore everybody listens to him willingly."

Hold a conversation with mutual trust.

> Confucius said, "It is a wise conversation when you strive to understand the person with whom you talk, not only without distrusting him, but also without considering his distrust of you."

Surely, we should start a dialogue with mutual trust. If we speak with one another while not trusting each other, we will not speak frankly and the conversation will be meaningless. On the other hand, if we begin a conversation with trust between us, we will speak frankly, so that even if one of us lies it will become apparent.

Make the most effective use of a meeting

Talk at the right time.

> Confucius said, "Everyone will pay attention if you talk at the right time. You are considered hasty if you talk before you should. You will waste your words if you talk when you should not."

Listen to every opinion in a meeting.

> Confucius said, "A Gentleman neither evaluates a person only by words nor rejects the words of someone who is underestimated."

Speak concisely in a meeting.

> Confucius said, "A Gentleman is so clever that he dislikes subsidiary words before saying essential ones."

> "The function of words is only to communicate."

Surely he is a good businessman who listens to every opinion carefully, regardless of who speaks.

Reach a conclusion to a meeting within a given time.

> Confucius said, "Those who meet and talk throughout the day without any significant conclusion find it difficult to do anything useful."

Today's good businessmen surely respect the time that is spent with others in conference.

Give and accept advice carefully

Give advice positively, but not persistently.

> Tze Lu asked how to serve his superior. Confucius answered, "Advise him even if you are opposed by him. Not to advise him is to betray him." Tze Kung asked how to associate with friends. Confucius answered, "Be earnest in advising friends. But as soon as you feel their disgust, you have to stop the advice." Tze Yu, one of the youngest disciples, said, "Advice too persistent to a superior may seem like an insult. Advice too persistent to friends alienates the adviser from his friends."

Direct, tough advice can rub others the wrong way, even if the advice is appropriate. In this case, it is wrong to come straight to the point. Instead, one should be careful to advise others, including subordinates and others close to them, as indirectly and gently as possible.

On the other hand, if one receives gentle advice, then one should ask the meaning of the advice so that it can be understood and one can reform oneself exactly according to the advice.

Accept advice exactly.

> Confucius said, "Accept proper advice from famous sayings obediently. Strive to reform yourself immediately according to it. Accept indirect, gentle advice willingly after confirming what it really means. I cannot do anything for those who do not reform according to advice, nor ask what advice means."

Advise differently, depending upon the person whom you advise.

> Confucius said, "Good for one case may not be good for another."

> A disciple asked Confucius, "Must I do right away what I regard as good?" Confucius replied, "No, do it after listening to your father and brother." Another disciple asked the same question. Confucius replied, "Yes, do it as soon as possible." The third disciple, who had heard the two conversations, asked Confucius, "Why did you change your answer?" Confucius replied, "I pull one backward because he is too active, while I push the other forward because he is too passive."

If we speak without regard for the standpoint of others, no one will listen. We should strive to advise and persuade others with words that are tailored to the person we want to advise. We should clearly be aware of what and to whom we speak.

Know what should not be spoken

Do not speak of the past persistently.

> Confucius argued with an impertinent disciple: "Do not speak persistently about matters that are past. Do not object to deeds already done. Do not place blame for errors already committed."

> A hermit regarded Confucius as a man who talked only of the past, and said to him in a carriage, "Do not talk of the past. Discuss only the future." Confucius got off the carriage to discuss, but the hermit ran away.

Specifically, a Gentleman dislikes these people: one who complains of his own deed, which has brought on failure; a senior who advises his subordinates by always referring to the same examples; a teacher who argues with his pupils, quoting an argument of which they are already well aware; and a manager who incessantly reminds his workers of their mistakes, even though the workers have admitted them.

Neither backbite nor criticize others.

> Seeing Tze Kung, the talkative disciple, criticizing others, Confucius said, "I have no time to criticize others." Tze Kung asked Confucius whom a gentleman should shun. Confucius answered, "Those who secretly attack the character or deeds of others should be shunned."

Regardless of how persistently we criticize others, they will not reform themselves. We should therefore not criticize others.

Blame yourself instead of others.

> Confucius said, "Hidden wrongs will be eliminated if you blame yourself instead of others."

Behind every wrong are many unknown wrongs. Instead of criticizing others, criticize yourself. If you openly criticize yourself for similar faults, others will then reform themselves voluntarily.

Do not pretend intelligence.

> Tsang, the successor to Confucius as a scholar, said, "I reflect often, even daily upon whether I have passed on what I have not studied deeply."

An expert who transfers only others' knowledge is a mere scholar; a mere scholar is but mere mass.

Association

Important Sayings:

Throughout his life, Confucius did not forget loyalty to and consideration for others.

Do not ask others to do what you do not want to do yourself.

A Gentleman who serves well in an organization places himself below others.

Humility based on good manners incurs no dishonor.

Do nothing—not watching, speaking or listening—without polite manners.

You cannot play your proper role if you do not understand what polite manners are.

Never make your parents worry over you, except in the case of your illness.

How pleasant it is to welcome friends who come from far away!

A Gentleman works with others, but joins no specific faction.

The Master of *Jin* resents no one, either in his business or in his home.

A virtuous person is not left alone. He is sure to make many good friends.

Have consideration for others

Have consideration for and loyalty to others.

> Tsang said, "Through his life, Confucius did not forget loyalty and consideration for others."
>
> Confucius asked Yen Hui, the virtuous disciple, about his creed. Yen Hui answered, "I will never boast of my merits to others, nor make difficulties for others."
>
> Tze Kung, the clever disciple, asked, "Is there a deed expressed with a few words that everyone should try to do throughout their lives?" Confucius answered, "This is 'consideration for others.' Do not ask others to do what you do not want to do yourself."
>
> Tze Kung came to Confucius and pledged, "I will never force others to do what I do not want others to force me to do." Confucius knew that Tze Kung was being argumentative rather than practical, and told him, "I am afraid that pledge is too difficult for you. But make up your mind firmly to do it."

It is very difficult for modern intellectuals to practice these teachings because they love to argue. They enjoy such arguments as "It is competition that makes a country progress," and "The competition should be carried out by ignoring others."

Consider others' promotion and success before your own.

> Confucius said, "The Master of *Jin* works to have others promoted before he is promoted. The Master of *Jin* works to have others achieve before he does."

During the era of Confucius, called the Warlike Age, many countries fought one another. In Confucius' country, three lords were grasping for hegemony, under a king who acted only as a figurehead. Thus, the above quotation of Confucius' was only a theoretical idea and was not practiced.

Similarly, people today compete everywhere. Statesmen compete for votes in elections. Students compete in entrance exams. Companies compete with other companies for market shares. It's as though people consider nothing to be as important as winning.

As a result, it sometimes happens that a salesman who wins in a game against his customer will lose the order, and a manager who is promoted faster than others will lose his popularity just after his promotion. In the broader sense, a winner is sometimes the loser, and vice versa.

Take care of others.

> Confucius said, "A Gentleman who serves well in an organization takes good care of others."

Show respect for others by your attitude

Put yourself after others, with proper manners.

> Confucius said, "A Gentleman who serves well in an organization places himself after others."
>
> Tze Yu said, "Humility based on good manners incurs no dishonor."
>
> Confucius said, "A writer wrote in his essay that practicing humility with flattering talk and patronizing manners incurs dishonor. I agree with him."

Never be arrogant.

> Confucius said, "A Gentleman is calm without arrogance, while a vagrant is arrogant without composure."

> Tze Kung said, "A Gentleman shuns rude people who consider arrogance a form of courage."

Arrogance is the worst attitude in breaking human connections. We should strive always to keep away from being arrogant.

Never ignore or disdain others.

> Confucius said, "A Gentleman does not disdain anything, whether it is great or small. He does not make little of his opponents, whether they are many or few. Thus, he always has good composure without haughtiness."

> "It is easy not to be disdainful when one is rich. On the other hand, it is difficult not to be resentful when one is poor."

It is easy for a Gentleman not to disdain others, because he is rich—at least in spirit.

People gather around a Gentleman because he disdains no one.

> In order to cheer up a disciple of Confucius who had lost his brother, another disciple said to him, "A Gentleman ignores or despises nothing. Instead, he is prudent, careful, and well-mannered so that everyone in the world is his brother. You are a Gentleman so that you need not worry about not having blood-related brothers."

Keep polite manners

Do nothing without polite manners.

> Yen Hui asked about *Jin*. Confucius answered, "Do
> nothing—neither watching, speaking, nor listening—
> without polite manners." Yen Hui pledged to keep this
> throughout his life.

Understand the meaning of manners.

> Confucius said, "You cannot play your proper role if you
> do not understand what polite manners are."

> "Humility without politeness leads to servility. Prudence
> without politeness leads to timidity. Bravery without
> politeness leads to coarseness. Honesty without politeness
> leads to heartlessness."

I think that Confucius was here defining mankind as an animal that behaves with manners. I know that other definitions
for mankind exist (for instance, that man is an animal that uses
tools, or he is a social animal). But other animals make and use
tools, and some live in social units. I agree with the definition
Confucius offers here.

Practice politeness with those persons closest to you.

> Yu Tzu, the disciple who was respected because he
> resembled Confucius, said, "A harmonious association is
> at its best when based on polite manners. It is impossible
> to keep a harmonious association without polite manners,
> regardless of one's earnest."

A lord asked how to make use of people. Confucius answered, "A great manager directs his people politely."

Confucius said, "Please note that a manager is regarded by his employees as a flattering person who complements his superior, even if he serves his superior with good manners."

There is a Japanese proverb that says we need politeness even among the closest association. Although I do not know of any proverbs from other countries concerning politeness, I think it is a universal truth that harmonious relations do not last without polite manners. We should practice politeness, even with those closest to us, such as family or co-workers. A good manager, aware of this principle, is polite to his subordinates.

Take the mental part of courtesy seriously.

A man asked about courtesy. Confucius responded, "Show courtesy in ceremonies and observe them moderately, even though these occasions tend to be sumptuous."

Confucius said, "Is it true that people think a gift is a courtesy with which to express thanks? I do not think so. They often confuse it with tribute."

It is regrettable, but the richer a country becomes the more sumptuous become its ceremonies, such as wedding receptions or funerals, thus violating Confucius' teaching. There is a custom in Japan in which a person sends gifts at the end of the year to those to whom he is indebted as a way of expressing thanks. Japanese people also bring gifts whenever they visit others' homes. This custom is meaningful so long as the spiritual aspects are recognized more than the gift itself. However, I'm afraid that the richer Japanese society becomes the more a gift becomes regarded for its competitive value. Consequently, the gift's outward appearance is thought more important than its spiritual significance. Confucius observed this more than two thousand years ago.

Get along with parents and children

Know that your parents are always at your side.

> Confucius said, "Whether talented or not, every parent cares for his child."

Take good care of your parents.

> A man asked about filial duty. Confucius answered, "Never make your parents worry over you, except in case of your illness."

> Confucius said, "Always keep the age of your parents in mind as a source of both happiness and anxiety."

Have affection for parents.

> Tze Yu, the writer, asked about filial duty. Confucius answered, "Recently, people regard filial duty as the support of their old parents. But, then, they support horses and gods as well. Without respect and affection for one's parents, one is said not to perform filial duty."

> Tze Hsia also asked about filial duty, and Confucius answered, "Filial duty requires that we express

spontaneous affection for our parents. Just to carry their heavy bags and serve them the best portions for dinner first is not filial duty."

Keep your distance from your grown-up children.

Confucius kept a distance between himself and his son at his school.

Teach hardship to your children.

Confucius taught his disciples, "If you love your children, then teach them hardship."

Understand the niceties of the heart

Know the spell of love.

A lover says in a song: "Petals are falling from a cherry tree waving in the breeze. I want to go to you becoming a petal, but your home is so far away." Confucius commented, "He does not really love her. If he did, there would be no distance between them."

Treat maids and menial servants wisely.

Confucius complained, "Maids and menial servants are difficult to deal with because they become arrogant if we become too close to them, while they hate us if we keep them at a distance."

This saying exemplifies the grief Confucius felt when he was forced, as a man of high salary, to employ maids and servants in his fifties.

Cherish friendship

Develop meaningful friendships and enjoy them.

> Confucius said, "How pleasant it is to welcome friends who come from far away."

> Confucius said, "There are three useful pleasures: to have many good friends, to enjoy music moderately, and to talk of the merits of others."

> Tsang said, "A Gentleman meets with friends to learn and enjoy cultural things with them. Thus, he increases his understanding of humanity."

Keep everlasting friendships with old friends.

> The Great Duke of Chou said, "Long acquaintances should not be abandoned without an overwhelming reason."

> Confucius said, "A manager's respectful treatment of his old acquaintances makes his employees warmhearted."

> Confucius praised a famous administrator, saying, "A good administrator has good associations with many people and continues to be respectful toward friends, even after a long acquaintance with them."

Have a good network of friends

Make friendships that are suitable.

> Confucius taught his disciples, "Do not have friendships with those who are unsuitable for you."

I have heard that someone in the Republic of China argued with Confucius that one is not a Gentleman who selects friends according to his own likes and dislikes. I agree with Confucius, because I think that not only occurs, but also people too noble, too rich, or sometimes too wise are not friends suitable for me.

Have useful friendships.

> Confucius said, "It is useful to have a friend who is honest, loyal, and very knowledgeable. It is not useful to have a friend who is superficial, inconsistent, and flattering."

Do not try to be everyone's friend.

> Confucius said, "Those who pretend to be virtuous by speaking sweet words, even to bad fellows, are the enemies of virtue."

> Tze Kung asked, "Is he a good person who is loved by all of his neighbors?" Confucius replied, "Not necessarily." Tze Kung asked further, "Is he a good person who is shunned by his neighbors?" Confucius answered, "No, it is the best person who is loved by good neighbors and shunned by bad ones."

Today there are salespeople who will say "yes" to everyone in order to make a sale, or statesmen who talk sweet words to everyone just to get votes. These people would have been disliked by Confucius.

Extend friendship without favoritism.

> Confucius said, "A Gentleman works with others, but joins no special faction.

Join no faction.

> Confucius said, "A Gentleman works with others, but joins no special factions."

A Gentleman can extend the friendship of justice.

> Confucius said, "A Gentleman has neither hostility against anyone nor over-concern for things already done. Therefore, he can associate with all just people."

> "A virtuous person is not left alone. He is sure to make many good friends."

Shun vice, but resent no one

Abhor what you think to be wrong.

> Tze Kung asked Confucius whether a Gentleman eschews others or not. Confucius replied, "Yes, he shuns someone.

He shuns those who backbite, those who slander a superior, those who are brave with ill manners, and those who insist unyieldingly." Then Confucius asked Tze Kung's opinion. Tze Kung replied, "A Gentleman shuns those who are not brave being ill-mannered, those who pretend to be intelligent by telling second-hand information, and those who pretend to be honest by exposing others' faults."

Understand that resentment is the worst sentiment.

Chung Kung, the disciple Confucius expected to be a statesman, asked about *Jin*. Confucius answered, "The Master of *Jin* resents no one in his business or his home."

There are many teachings by Asian sages, such as Buddha, Confucius, and Lao-tze, that instruct that resentment is the worst sentiment for human relations.

Know how to avoid resentment.

Confucius said, "Continuing to blame a person eventually induces resentment against him."

"Those who blame themselves more severely than others will incur no resentment."

"A Gentleman does not think of wrong deeds done by others. Hence, he usually is free from resentment."

I like these Japanese maxims that lead us to avoid resentment: "To forgive what one can never forgive is to forgive," and "Wash your hate with water as soon as possible."

Do not associate with those whom you resent.

> Confucius said, "A writer states in his essay that he has been ashamed of friendships with those he resents. I want to follow him."

Since a Gentleman is not the Master of *Jin,* the ideal person, he may sometimes resent others. In this case, he avoids persons whom he resents, because it is shameful for him to have a superficial friendship.

Return honesty for resentment.

> Confucius said, "A Gentleman returns honesty for resentment and virtue for virtue."

It sometimes happens that a Gentleman is forced to contact people he resents. In this case, he tries to show honesty instead of hostility and never plays on them. There is a well-known saying of Lao-tze that a Gentleman returns virtue for resentment. However, I think that this opinion is too simple.

MANAGEMENT

Important Sayings:

A leader must bear the entire responsibility for the faults of his followers.

The will cannot be taken from the humblest man while the captain-general can be taken even from the largest army.

If a manager has neatness in his clothing and gravity in his appearance, he will earn respect from his employees.

You cannot move your people unless you are polite, however great your knowledge, virtue, or dignity.

Generosity is welcome by people and fairness makes them happy.

If a leader takes good care of his closest people, his people will act according to *Jin*.

Begin management with clear definitions of technical terms.

You can activate your business if you use competent people in important jobs and instruct the less able by yourself.

You will spoil our people if you employ them in difficult tasks before training them.

A Gentleman praises a person on his merit in order to develop it further.

We cannot tell whether a person is either great or superficial, no matter how appealing his speech may be.

To know a person you must know his creed.

Establish mutual trust before all else

Gain trust of superiors and subordinates alike before everything.

> Confucius said, "The person who lacks confidence cannot do anything useful."

> Confucius said, "A Gentleman employs his people seriously only after being trusted. Without trust, the workers may think that they are being ill-used. A Gentleman gives advice to his superior only after earning trust from him; otherwise the superior may feel some criticism in his advice."

You cannot manage even neighbors unless you earn their trust with sincerity.

> Tzu Chang, the young disciple who wanted to be a manager, asked about management. Confucius answered, "Management by loyal and reliable words and sincere acts is welcome even by people with different culture. On the contrary, management that lacks trust and sincerity can do nothing effective, even in your hometown."

> Confucius said, "Your people will rely on you if there is mutual trust between management and labor."

Establish unity with fairness

Manage people with fairness.

> Confucius said, "Fairness makes people happy."

Establish unity with fairness.

> When a king whom Tze Lu, the bravest disciple, served
> planned a war to conquer a neighbor, Tze Lu came to
> Confucius and told him of the plan. Confucius scolded
> Tze Lu for having not remonstrated with the king and
> said, "The administrator who keeps his country well is
> concerned with fairness, but not so much with a small
> salary. He worries about instability of administration but
> little about a small number of people." Confucius
> continued, "Fair treatment of people eliminates
> dissatisfaction of a small salary. Unity of people covers
> anxiety of a small number of them. Thus, people rely on
> the country. If they rely on it wholeheartedly, then the
> country will never decline." Then Confucius urged Tze Lu
> to advise his king to stop the plans for war at once.

I am sorry that Saddam Hussein and his administration in
Iraq did not learn this lesson.

Have generosity, virtue, and dignity

Be generous toward people and serious toward management.

> Confucius said, "Generosity is welcomed by employees."

> Confucius said, to Tzu Chang, a disciple who wanted to
> be a manager, "I believe that a manager who is neither
> generous nor polite can do nothing effective."

> When Confucius was thinking that a person too exact was
> not qualified as a leader, a disciple of Confucius who
> administered some land came and asked Confucius

whether his lord was great or not. Confucius, who had heard that the lord was generous, replied instantly, "Yes, he is qualified to be a leader because he is generous." Responding to Confucius' opinion, the disciple said, "Generosity is always necessary for a leader, but it is not enough. If a leader is not prudent, then he cannot lead people, however generous he is." Confucius agreed.

Always be virtuous.

Confucius said, "A virtuous manager can extend good leadership as if all other stars turn toward the north star, which keeps its place."

Strive to cultivate dignity.

Confucius said, "People do not respect a manager unless he has dignity and seriousness, even if he has both knowledge and virtue."

Have neatness in clothing to earn dignity.

Confucius said, "If a manager is neat in his clothing and serious in his appearance, he will earn the dignity of his people."

Treat subordinates carefully

Treat subordinates politely.

> Confucius said, "You cannot lead your people unless you are mannerly, however great are your knowledge, virtue, and dignity."

> Chung Kung asked about *Jin*. Confucius answered, "Use your people politely, as if you were a master of great ceremony."

Take good care of your people.

> Confucius said, "If a manger takes good care of his closest people, then his people will act according to *Jin*."

Use competent persons without favoritism.

> Confucius said to Chung Kung, "An ox with magnificent horns and wonderful skin color, even if used in the low labor of farming, will soon be promoted to divine use. The ox will be discovered by the supreme existence that governs mountains and rivers, even if the farmer tries to hide it."

> When Tzu Yu, the youngest disciple, was made a minister of state, he came to Confucius and praised one of his men: "He dislikes to come to my office without official business."

> Confucius reflected: "I did not abuse or praise a particular person in front of many people. It is only when I had a special intention that I praised a person."

Lead with clear words and examples

Define technical terms clearly.

> When Tze Lu asked Confucius what to do if management
> was in disorder, Confucius replied, "Begin management
> with clear definitions of technical terms." Tze Lu said, "I
> understand why they say you are too slack." Confucius
> scolded him: "Hold your tongue! It is a Gentleman who
> never speaks what he does not know exactly. People
> cannot respond to orders, so the leader can do nothing so
> long as he uses unclear words."

Technology today has given us numerous technical terms in a
field, such as computer, semiconductor, biotechnology, etc.
Moreover, system engineering and software engineering are
developing many new terms that seem indefinite and unclear.
Leaders in the engineering fields particularly should make extra
effort to define new technical terms clearly, asking for help
from their people. Otherwise, they cannot lead their people to
better achievements.

Do not issue vague orders.

> Tzu Chang asked about management. Confucius replied,
> "It is the worst leader who, with rude orders, expects
> outstanding results from his people. It is the lowest type of
> leader who requires only good results from his people
> without giving them explicit advice."

Initiate important tasks.

> Tze Lu, when assigned a post as administrator in the country, asked Confucius how to direct people. Confucius replied, "Take the initiative in the important tasks for your organization and show by example." Tze Lu asked further and Confucius replied, "Never tire in taking the initiative."

I can illustrate the meaning of "taking the initiative" with an example. A project team developing a new product consists of a leader and several specialists (called a "collective genius"). If the team is working on a truly creative idea, they can certainly expect to come up against barriers on the way to success. The team leader must take the initiative to find ways either to break down these barriers or to find a roundabout way to get the idea accepted. The leader must be able to predict the barriers before they are encountered, and foresee ways of eliminating or getting around the barriers. In short, the leader must take the initiative in advancing the team beyond the barriers.

Employ all people effectively and rely on them

Employ all of your people effectively.

> Tzu Chang said, "A Gentleman makes use of all of his people. He leaves no one out of the process. He appreciates the competent ones and gives them important jobs, while he guides the less competent." He added, "If I am a Gentleman and wise, there is none whom I cannot lead."

> A manager asked how to activate his business. Confucius replied, "You can activate your business if you use

competent people in important jobs and instruct the less able yourself."

A manager should take care to guide the less competent himself. More precisely, a manager should instruct the less competent directly in order to raise their abilities to a level where he can make suitable use of their skills and assign them to appropriate tasks. Failure to assign suitable work to some people will cause them to complain about being misused, and that can lead to the demoralization of the entire organization.

Make every effort to give everyone his proper job.

> Tzu Chang asked about management. Confucius answered, "People respect a Gentleman even if he uses that person hard. A Gentleman always strives to give his people the proper job, taking their requests into consideration, if necessary. Who can be disrespectful of the Gentleman?"

Don't try to control everything.

> A state official asked Confucius about farming. Confucius refused to reply. After the man went away, Confucius said, "Any old farmer knows more about farming than I. Why did he ask me about farming, disregarding his own role? He should be interested in the administration of the people."

> Tsang said, "A manager should not comment on the tools for sacrifice. He should leave it up to the person in charge, and concentrate instead on how to celebrate the festival as a whole."

Confucius said, "A Gentleman does not interfere in his people's affairs."

Develop the abilities of employees

Train your people before you put them to difficult tasks.

Confucius said, "You will spoil your people if you use them in difficult tasks before training them properly."

Train your people through discussion.

Confucius said, "Do I have any particular knowledge to impart? No, I don't. When a person requires me to teach, I first examine whether he is sincere. If so, the only thing I do is to point out ambiguous points and discuss these thoroughly and in detail."

"I discuss with my disciples frankly and tell them of all I know. Then I try to put the conclusion of the discussion into practice, together with them."

Understand the limits of education.

Confucius said, "It is impossible to make all of your people understand all about management. But it is possible to make your people work as you want."

Develop the talents of your people through work.

Confucius said, "A Gentleman praises a person on his merit in order to develop them further."

Confucius said, "A good manager makes people an excellent instrument once he makes use of them."

A good manager knows that the successful completion of a job develops a person's abilities, and vice versa. Therefore, a good manager gives suitable work to his employees. In the course of time, the employees succeed and the manager praises his people. Thus, the employees have developed self-confidence, and this self-confidence challenges the employees on to new tasks and higher challenges.

Evaluate a person totally, considering his age

Evaluate people from several points of view.

Confucius said, "To know a person you must know his creed."

Confucius said, "You cannot understand a person if you do not know his words."

Confucius said, "It is sure that the person who possesses virtue speaks good words, but not vice versa."

Confucius said, "We cannot tell whether a person is great or superficial, however appealing his speech."

Confucius said, "You will know all about a man if you examine his vision, his motives, and his cause."

Confucius said, "It is in the cold of winter that you find out that pines and firs are evergreens."

Expect a bright future for young persons.

> Confucius said, "Never see a limit in the future of a young person. The future of a young person cannot be predicted from his present state."

Be careful in promoting a young person early.

> Tze Lu promoted a young man to an important position too early. Confucius said, "The young man may be spoiled." Tze Lu objected: "On-the-job training is the most important. Why should I give him the position only after making him learn from books and many superiors?" Confucius mumbled, "I hate the fluent tongue of Tze Lu."

You can still evaluate a person past forty.

> Confucius said, "People do not respect those who have achieved no reputation until forty or fifty."

> Confucius said, "If a person is disliked by many past forty, he is not an able person."

Confucius believed that a person usually reaches his potential by the age of forty, and he thought that a person older than fifty who lost the trust of his fellows and was disliked could not perform his duties adequately.

ADMINISTRATION

Important Sayings:

If we lack confidence, then we cannot do anything right.

A Gentleman thinks of justice first, while a mean person is always concerned with profits.

First consider what you can do for customers, and then think of the remuneration.

A Gentleman is honest, but not senselessly honest.

If a manager pleases people close to him, then those far from him will come willingly to join with him.

Do not seek perfection in a person when you employ him.

Enrich your company first, then think of how to educate your people.

A Gentleman is neither stingy nor extravagant.

Without a long-range plan, you will run into trouble in the short term.

A quick accomplishment results in a prominent achievement.

Carry out a task after reviewing it twice; three times is too much.

Good in one case may not be good in another.

Challenge an ambitious target with your full effort. If you fail, quit your post.

Respect trust above all

Trust is essential.

> Confucius said, "If we lack confidence, then we cannot do anything right."

> Tzu Chang asked about administration. Confucius replied, "People never recognize a company that has no trust."

> Yu Tzu said, "Unless you make a contract based on mutual trust and social justice, it will never be carried out smoothly."

> Tze Kung asked Confucius what his politics were. Confucius replied, "It is to provide people food, protect people with armaments, and gain trust from people." Tze Kung asked further, "Which should we abandon first if our country is forced to abandon food, weapons, or trust?" Confucius replied, "Abandon weapons first, then food. But never abandon trust. People cannot get on without trust. Trust is more important than life. More people can be born, but trust is never regained."

Get a client's confidence before all else.

> Confucius drove to the Rain Altar on a holiday. Fan Chih, the youngest disciple, asked how to raise his virtue. Confucius answered, "First consider what you can do for clients, then think of the remuneration."

Maintain general ethics to earn other's trust.

> Confucius taught Tzu Lu: "Think of justice in the face of profits. Acts aimed only at profit induce all sorts of hate."

Confucius said, "A Gentleman thinks of justice first, while a mean person is always concerned only with profits."

Act as a manager of high standing

Exercise every possible effort in administration.

> Tzu Lu, who had been made a government official, asked Confucius what administration is. Confucius answered, "Do everything in your power tirelessly and execute everything with loyalty."

The top management must always be ethical.

> Confucius said, "If a manager is upright, his people play their roles correctly, even if he gives no orders. If not, people do not play their roles correctly, no matter what he says."

Do not be senselessly honest.

> Confucius said, "A Gentleman is honest, but not senselessly so."
>
> Tze Hsia said, "Important ethics should never be violated, while some trivial ethics can be ignored."
>
> Tze Lu said, "Do not violate general ethics while being concerned with private innocence."

Understand difficulties of top management.

> The king of his native country asked Confucius, "What behavior by a king destroys his country?" Confucius

replied, "A king destroys his country if his only pleasure is to see his people say nothing contrary to what he has said. If what he said is right, his country may be safe. However, if what he said is wrong, he will destroy his country." The king asked further about the good administrator and the good people who make his country prosperous. Confucius answered, "It is the good administrator who understands the difficulty of the role of his people. Likewise, it is the good people who understand the difficulty of the role of the administrator."

Confucius said, "If their country is administered well, people will speak actively and act honestly. If not, they obey silently."

One of the difficulties facing top management today is the fear subordinates have of telling their superiors what they think the superior does not want to hear. The subordinates are apt to think that "silence is golden." Managers, therefore, should always listen to their subordinates with a positive attitude and sincerity, no matter how bitter the opinions may be. Managers should remember that "good medicine is bitter only in the mouth."

Strengthen human resources

Gather as many competent people as possible.

When Confucius visited a land where one of his disciples was a minister of state, Confucius praised him: "How many people you have gathered!" When another disciple became a minister, Confucius asked him first, "Do you get able people?"

The fact that Japanese management does not generally lay off employees may come from this teaching of Confucius.

Know that people want to join a good company.

When a lord asked Confucius to tell something about administration, Confucius replied, "If a manager pleases people close to him, then those far away will come willingly to join with him."

Overlook slight weaknesses in your people.

The Great Duke of Chou said, "Do not seek perfection in a person when you first employ him."

Confucius said, "The inferior manager hopes for too much when he employs a person."

Confucius told one of his disciples, "Promote a person of talent, pardoning his past slight failure." The disciple asked him how he could find competent employees. Confucius said, "First list the names of those whom you know well, neglecting their past slight mistakes. As for those you do not know, others will recommend many in response to your request because they recognize what type of a person you want."

Employ radical and conservative workers.

Confucius said, "A well-balanced person is the best, but we seldom see such a person. Therefore, first seek a well-balanced person. If not possible, take a passionate person or an assertive person. Use him effectively, although the

former might be too aggressive and the latter too
stubborn."

Employ managers who understand your vision correctly.

A lord came to Confucius and asked how to realize his
vision. Confucius answered, "If you have managers who
understand your vision correctly, your employees will
understand your vision from them; otherwise, people will
not realize your principle."

Increase assets, but do not be stingy

Enrich your company by making profits.

Confucius drove around with a disciple who was a
minister of the state they were in. Confucius asked, "Do
you have good people?" The disciple replied, "Yes, I have.
What should I do next?" Confucius replied, "Enrich your
state first, then think how to educate your people."

A man praised a famous rich man: "Since he gains profits
justly, he is not disliked." Confucius nodded.

Evaluate your assets reservedly.

Confucius praised a famous businessman. "He says that
his company has very few assets when it earns them at
first. He says that his company has a few assets when it
earns them to a fair degree. He says that his company has
only a fair degree of assets when it earns them to a
considerable degree."

98

Generally speaking, Japanese businessmen speak and think conservatively about accumulation of their company's assets.

Be neither stingy nor extravagant.

> Confucius said, "A Gentleman is neither stingy nor extravagant."

> A government official rebuilt a warehouse. A disciple of Confucius criticized the official: "The old warehouse met its purposes adequately. Why did he then rebuild the warehouse?" Confucius praised the disciple. "Although he is a man of few words, his words are always to the point."

> Confucius said, "An extravagant or stingy person is never a good administrator, even if his talent is outstanding, like the Great Duke of Chou, in all other points."

> Confucius said, "To be unwilling to pay money that must be spent eventually is the mind-set only of a petty official, not a minister."

To enrich a company's assets, all members of the company must practice frugality. However, management should not confuse frugality with stinginess. The company that spends stingily can only diminish. One must understand the distinction between stinginess and frugality: Stinginess is not spending money that must be spent, while frugality is not wasting money on superficial things. Extravagance is not frugality.

Make investments based on sound planning

Make a long-range plan.

Confucius said, "Without a long-range plan, you will run into trouble in the short term."

In seeing a plan come to fruition, a certain time lag is inevitable. For example, it takes several months to realize an investment plan. If management makes an investment based only on current circumstances, without looking forward to possible changes in circumstances, then the investment will be affected by what has occurred after the time lag. If this lack of forward planning continues, then the company will have to deal with instability. In other words, long-range planning is indispensable to the management of an organization. Long-range planning is for the present, not the future.

Aim at great achievements without haste.

> When Tze Hsia was made a minister of state, he asked about administration. Confucius answered, "Do not expect accomplishments in too short a time. Do not adhere to small achievements. Concern for small achievements makes you lose great ones. Haste makes great achievements escape from you."

Provide your people with a good working environment.

> Confucius said, "A Gentleman uses resources positively and effectively for his organization."

Confucius said, "A high level of technology is attained only with the best possible tools."

Tzu Hsia said, "Good work is achieved only in a good and proper workplace."

Confucius said, "The Great King Yu spent more money on the public areas than on his office."

Work quickly and with flexibility

Accomplish a task as fast as possible.

Tzu Chang asked about administration. Confucius replied, "A quick accomplishment results in a prominent achievement."

Confucius said, "A Gentleman seeks rapid accomplishment of a task."

The quicker a task is accomplished, the better is the control of management or the system.

Accomplish even the greatest task within three years.

Confucius said, "I can accomplish a large project within one year on the average, and within three years at the longest."

This saying expresses today's standard of quickness for Japanese management.

Do not waste time in reviewing a plan.

> Confucius said, "Carry out a task after reviewing it twice. Three times is too much."

Be flexible at all times.

> Confucius said, "Good in one case may not be good in another case."

> A hermit who took Confucius for a rigid man told Confucius to be more flexible by making use of the following metaphor: "Raise your skirts when crossing a shallow river, and take off all your clothes when crossing a great river." Confucius responded, "Being flexible is too obvious to note it especially."

Confucius wanted to say that the manager who can show natural flexibility daily is qualified as a good manager.

Gather correct information

Gather information without bias.

> Confucius taught Tzu Chang: "First examine as many things as possible, abandon things that are doubtful, and finally talk prudently about those things. Then you are free from error."

> Confucius said, "It is important to check important information. For example, when someone informs you that a person is such and such, you should confirm for yourself whether it is true or not."

Ignore rumors and complaints.

Tzu Chang asked how to make administration clear. Confucius answered, "A wise manager ignores slanderous rumors and superficial complaints."

Know that no smoke rises without fire.

Confucius said, "People have arguments about an administration unless it is carried out well."

Be cautious of illness in a business

Beware of betrayals.

When Confucius stayed in a foreign city, the mayor praised a son who had disclosed his father's crime. Confucius said, "In our country, people do not regard such a deed as honest. People think it is an honest deed for a father to conceal the guilt of his son and vice versa."

Confucius had a discussion with Tze Kung, the most clever disciple. Confucius asked Tze Kung what he hated the most. Tze Kung replied, "I hate those who call themselves honest by disclosing their companions' wrongs."

Dr. Kaizuka said in his book, "I would like to forget a sorrowful story that occurred during the Chinese revolution. The Communist Party gave a prize to a son who had charged his father with being a spy." In any case, if any direct charge from inside the organization is made, a manager should consider it to be evidence of an illness in his organization.

Never be too concerned with keeping your post.

> Tzu Lu asked how to serve his superior. Confucius
> answered, "Advise your superior, even if you are opposed
> to him. Not to advise him is to betray him."
>
> Confucius taught Tzu Chang: "Challenge an ambitious
> target with your full effort. If you fail, quit your post."
>
> Confucius said, "It is a waste of time to work together
> with the mean person who complains of not getting a high
> post before he gets it and is afraid to lose it after getting it.
> He may do anything wrong to keep his post."

I imagine that, when Confucius was a minister of state in his
native country, he saw many government officials who were
concerned with keeping their posts. Similarly, today we see
many such government officials and company managers who are
concerned primarily with keeping their jobs. We need the
teachings of Confucius today as much as we did when
Confucius lived.